AMERICANS AT SCHOOL

Anne Moss and Janet Williams

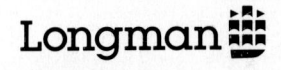

INTRODUCTION

Jodie is the oldest of three children in her family. She is nineteen years old, and she goes to college. She has always liked drawing and painting. Now, in college, she is learning to use her drawing and painting in ways that will help her get a good job.

Robert is Jodie's brother, two years younger than she is. He is still in high school. He has two interests: basketball and computers. Next year he will have to decide which college he wants to go to. The college with the best basketball team is not the one with the best classes in computers.

Sarah goes to elementary school. In fact, she goes to the same elementary school that her sister and her brother went to. She is eight years old and shows talent in many kinds of music. She takes piano lessons and likes to sing.

Before sending their children to school, the parents of Jodie, Robert, and Sarah had many questions. "How can we find a good school for our children?" "Will some students come from other neighborhoods?" "Does the school teach other languages besides English?" "Are the students all girls, or all boys?" "Are sports important?" "Does the school teach children with learning problems?" "Do the teachers belong to our church?" "Are private schools better than public ones?"

You will find some of the answers in this book.

Top left: Jodie.
Bottom left: Robert.
Above: Sarah.

ELEMENTARY SCHOOL: GRADES 1–6

American children go to elementary school when they are six years old and they stay there for six years. The school years are called "grades." The first year is the "first grade," and the last year is the "sixth grade." In most parts of the country, elementary schools also have kindergartens for five-year-olds.

Pre-schools are for children younger than five. In pre-school and kindergarten, children get ready for school. They play with other children and learn to listen to the teacher. These are important programs for young children.

American children do not have to go to school until age six, so not all children attend pre-school or kindergarten.

Public elementary schools usually have about 500 students. Boys and girls are in classes together, with between 15 and 30 other children. Some students learn fast. Others need extra help. Teachers may put pupils in small groups, where they can learn at different speeds.

Sarah spends most of her time in one classroom with her teacher, Mrs. Heller. Mrs. Heller teaches English (reading and writing), Mathematics, and Science. These

are the most important subjects. Sarah has to study Music, Art, French, and Health, too. But it's not all hard work at school. Sarah has time to go out for lunch, and to play. But Mrs. Heller gives her homework every night.

Mrs. Heller is a good teacher. Her classroom is comfortable. Her lessons are interesting. She teaches in an easy way without too many rules. Her students often raise their hands to ask questions and give answers. Good teachers like their students to learn actively and to think for themselves. They should be able to understand ideas, not just repeat what is in a book.

Left: Sarah's class and her teacher, Mrs. Heller.
Above: An art class.

HIGH SCHOOL: GRADES 7–12

Why must children go to school? That's an easy question. They must learn to read and write and do Math. Yes, but they must learn other important lessons, too. They must learn to make friends with boys and girls in their class. They must learn to choose, to use free time well, and to study alone. In junior high school (grades seven and eight) and in high school (grades nine through twelve) these are important lessons.

Robert is in eleventh grade. The first teacher he sees in the morning is his homeroom teacher. The homeroom teacher gives him information for the day. Then Robert goes to his first class. The teachers stay in their classrooms, while Robert and his friends go from class to class.

Robert must take the important subjects, but he may choose other subjects as well. Robert is good at History and French, so he chooses those subjects. A special teacher called a guidance counselor helps him to choose, and gives him help with other problems, too. Every high school student has a guidance counselor.

It's nice to be in high school because you have more free time.

The students use that free time in many different ways. Robert is on the high school basketball team, which plays after school. He has joined some clubs, too. He is a member of the computer club and the French club. Some of his friends with the same interests meet together after school. Two or three teachers and some of the parents help with the clubs.

Robert's friend Greg is a member of the camera club at school. He also plays the drums in the school band. When Robert and Greg are not busy with clubs, they go to the school library or to quiet study rooms. Learning to use free time well is an important part of high school life.

Left: Students on the way to their next class.
Above: Greg and his band.

SOCIAL LIFE

In American high schools, there is often as much interest in other students as there is in school subjects. You can see this when you look at a typical high school yearbook. It is written once a year by students in the twelfth grade. In the yearbook, there is a picture of each teacher and student. Other photos show teachers and students at football and basketball games, in class, at club meetings, or at school dances.

Choosing leaders is a large part of high school life. The children decide which students should direct school business and lead them in Student Council. This is a group of five or six students who talk to teachers about what happens at school. About once a month, some of the Student Council leaders go to a meeting of the PTSA (Parent Teacher Student Association). There they work with parents and teachers to make their school better.

For many students in American high schools, the important thing is making friends, being popular, and having a good social life. Many students go out together after school—to fast food restaurants, movies, or dances. One big social event that takes place in high schools is the "prom," or school dance. The students go to the prom in couples. The boys wear "tuxedos," and the girls wear beautiful dresses.

During the high school years, students make strong friendships. They remember high school friends and other students long after they have finished school. So every ten years they come together. They have a special party with others from their graduating class. The graduating class is all the students who finished school the same year. At that big class party, the students look at old yearbook photos and talk about what happened at school and what has happened since then. They often remember the high school years as the best years of their lives.

Far left: Yearbook photos from a California high school.
Left: A prom couple.

THE SCHOOL DAY

Sarah's day at elementary school

9:00 A.M. Sarah leaves home. The school is more than a mile and a half from her home, so the school bus picks her up. Classes start at 9:20.
11:00 A.M. Sarah is listening to her teacher. Soon she will write a lesson in her workbook. Her teacher knows that elementary school children can work well for only about thirty minutes at a time, so lessons last only thirty minutes. Between lessons, Sarah can play games, read, or go outside to play.
12:00 Sarah is in the lunchroom. She likes to eat the hot lunch she can buy there. Sometimes she eats her favorite foods—hamburgers, pizza, or spaghetti. The school often serves fish, chicken, fruit, and salad, too. Students can drink juice or milk. Sarah likes the lunchroom. It's noisy and friendly.
3:15 P.M. Sarah goes home with some friends.

Robert's day at high school

7:30 A.M. Robert leaves home and drives his family's car to school. The school has a parking lot for students who drive. Lessons start at 8:00.

11:00 A.M. Robert is in Math class. The class will last fifty minutes. Robert and all his friends take at least five subjects, but they do not have all their subjects every day. Most classes meet three times a week. There is usually time for five classes a day. That leaves four hours a week for study and fun.

12:00 Robert is having lunch in the cafeteria. He takes his own lunch to school in a lunch box.

2:35 P.M. Robert's school day is finished now. He can go and meet his friends at the nearest fast food restaurant. They spend time after school doing things they like: listening to music and talking to friends, meeting with club members, or playing on sports teams.

Top left: Sarah leaves for school on the school bus.
Bottom left: In the lunchroom.
Left: Robert arrives in the school parking lot.
Above: Robert in his Math class.

SPORTS IN SCHOOL

Americans learn sports as part of their education. They learn two or more ball games, such as football or basketball. At high school, they choose groups of boys or girls to make teams. They choose those who are best at that sport. These teams compete against teams from other schools. In many schools students learn wrestling, running, tennis, golf and swimming. They have teams for some of these sports, too.

Robert's high school basketball team is very good. They have won the most games against other high school basketball teams in their state. Robert's parents, friends, and teachers all travel with the team to other schools to watch them play.

Robert's team practices often. The team meets every day after

school, and two Saturdays a month. Sometimes Robert wishes he had more time to meet with his friends, and he doesn't like getting up early on Saturdays. But most of the time he is happy to be on the team. He loves basketball, and he enjoys playing against other schools.

The games between schools are often very exciting. Other students, the ones not on the team, love to watch them. They like it if their team beats the other team. They let everyone know this by shouting and cheering when their team is playing well.

There is a special club of girls and boys (mostly girls) who jump up and down and shout for their football team. They call themselves cheerleaders, because they lead everyone in shouts and cheers. They wear clothes of a special color—the color of their school's team. The football players wear that color, too. Each school has a team color and a team name. Cheerleaders call out the team name in their cheers. They practice many hours to learn the special jumping and cheering. Cheerleading is almost a sport itself.

Left: Basketball.
Above: Cheerleaders.

CEREMONIES IN SCHOOL

Pledge of Allegiance

Every classroom has an American flag in it. From elementary to high school, students start each day by standing up and saluting the flag. They put their hands over their hearts and say the "Pledge of Allegiance." This is a promise to the country. It was written by people who came to America over 200 years ago. Saluting the flag helps people think about the United States and its freedoms.

Homecoming

At many high schools and universities there is a big football game once a year and a parade afterwards. This is called "Homecoming." Students who graduated from the school like to return for Homecoming to see their old friends and teachers again. In the parade cheerleaders and football players walk together. The school band plays loud music for their fans and team. The parade is full of the school colors.

Awards

In American schools there are ceremonies for students who have done good work in school or who are excellent at sports. At these special ceremonies all the students and teachers come together. They watch the school director give prizes to the students. Sometimes the prize is money for later university study.

Graduation

When students graduate from high school, each of them gets a prize. The prize they get is the high school diploma, written on nice paper with the name of the student and the school. Afterwards the graduating class has a big party, or "prom." Everyone wears fine clothes and a band plays dance music. It is a party to remember. Students, teachers, and parents have worked hard for each diploma. Graduation is the greatest ceremony of all in American schools.

Left: Second-grade students saying the Pledge of Allegiance.
Above: Graduation.

NEIGHBORHOOD SCHOOLS

There is no great difference between city, suburban, and country schools in the United States. Public schools teach the same subjects in the same grades across the land. Most school buildings look the same and have the same types of rooms inside. There is always a gym, a large room for basketball and other sports. There is a lunchroom, a school library, and an auditorium, a very large room where all the students and teachers can meet. Most schools also have rooms for the school band to practice in. They have rooms for students to type and use computers. There are usually rooms for students to work with paint, wood, metal, and other materials. These are all part of most American public schools, no matter where they are.

Each school serves a neighborhood, and neighborhoods *are* different. In some, the parents take an interest in what their children are doing at school. They give their time, their ideas, and they may give gifts to their schools.

That's what makes a good school in America. Generally, it doesn't matter whether the neighborhood is rich or poor, or whether it is in the city, the suburbs, or the country. What matters is the interest the neighborhood takes in its school.

Schools try to interest students in their neighborhood, too. Trips to the firehouse, police headquarters, newspaper offices, and other places are very popular with young children. Some schools have newspapers written by students for their neighbors. Older students may clean up the neighborhood together. They may earn money by washing cars, and use the money to help sick or elderly people in the neighborhood. These are ways students learn about the American way of life. They start with their neighborhood.

Left: A typical high school.
Above: Helping elderly people in New York.

17

PRIVATE SCHOOLS

Private does not mean better. But it does mean expensive. Public schools in the U.S. are paid for by money from everyone; private schools are not. Parents who send their children to private schools must pay to do so.

Parents may have enough money to pay for private school. But these schools do not have to accept their children. Most private schools accept only children who are already doing well in school and are able to work quietly. Some take only boys or only girls. Classes are often quieter and less crowded than classes in public schools. This gives children a chance to learn more of what their teachers are trying to teach them.

Public schools do not teach religion. So some parents choose private religious schools for their children. These schools each belong to a church. They give lessons about that religion. They give lessons in all the usual school subjects as well.

Children at many private schools wear special school uniforms, all exactly the same. At public schools, students wear what they want. They often dress in bright colors and tennis shoes. They sometimes invent new and wonderful fashions.

Only about 17 percent of American children are sent to private schools. Most Americans really believe in public education. They want their children to go to schools that are free and are open to all. They want their children to make friends with everyone— children of all races, from all kinds of families, with different talents, and different interests.

Left: Students on their way to a private girls' high school.

Above: A private elementary school.

BLACKS AND WHITES IN SCHOOL

Before the 1960s, black and white children did not go to the same schools. They did not usually eat at the same restaurants or sit together on buses. In 1955, a black woman, Rosa Parks, went to jail because she would not give her seat on a public bus to a white person. The blacks in her town got very angry and stopped riding the buses. Their black church leader, Martin Luther King Jr, helped them find other ways to travel to work. The buses lost money and some whites wanted to put King in jail. Instead, in 1956, the law changed. Blacks and whites could now sit together on public buses.

Another law was made saying that whites could not keep blacks out of their schools. In 1957, in Little Rock, Arkansas, nine black students tried to go to an all white high school. An angry crowd of whites did not let them enter. Special police had to come to the school. They guarded the black students as they entered the school. For months, they were there with guns when the children went to school in the morning.

Black people slowly began to win their fight for fairer laws. Some schools in black neighborhoods were too crowded. Black students from there went to less crowded

schools in white neighborhoods. They went on school buses. This started in the 1960s, and was called "bussing."

Especially at first, bussing caused a lot of problems for schools. Some students and their parents were angry. They didn't want students from a different neighborhood to come to their school. Sometimes the police had to stop students fighting.

In most parts of the country, blacks and whites now go to the same schools. Schools have both black and white teachers, as well. Relations between blacks and whites in America have changed a lot since the 1960s. You can see this most clearly in the schools, where black and white children and teachers now work together.

Left: Little Rock, Arkansas, 1957. Soldiers guard black high school students.

Above: Bussing in Boston in the early 1970s.

THE MELTING POT

Every American schoolchild learns that the United States is the big "melting pot" of countries. In a melting pot, different metals are melted together to make a new, stronger metal. The United States is like a melting pot for people. In the past, people from many different European countries came to the U.S. and made one country out of many.

Today people are still coming to live in the U.S. Most come from Latin America and from Asia. Of course, students like learning about the customs of the "old countries." In San Francisco, for example, there are many Chinese people. There the schools like to have a Chinese New Year's party.

Spanish is the language most people speak when they come to the United States. There are about two million Spanish-speaking children in American public schools today. Most of their classes are taught in Spanish. But they learn English every day, too. As they learn more English, they take more classes in English. The schools know that many parents of these children cannot read English. So most letters and information about school are written in both English and Spanish.

In Robert's class at high school there are several students whose parents came from other countries. Two students came to the U.S. when they were children. Emi's family came to the U.S. from Japan when she was ten. Emi hopes to stay in the U.S. and go to college next year when her family returns to Japan. Miguel is from Mexico. His mother came to work in the U.S. as a doctor two years ago. At first it was very difficult for Miguel to understand the lessons at school, but now he speaks English as well as everyone else.

If they stay in the U.S., Emi and Miguel will learn the English language, and they will learn about the American way of life. They will soon be as "American" as their classmates.

Top left: Learning to read in elementary school.

Bottom left: Celebrating Chinese New Year at a kindergarten.

Above: Robert's class in the library. Emi and Miguel are standing.

TESTS, MARKS, AND REPORT CARDS

Did you think that tests are only for students? You're wrong. The tests that students take also test their teachers and schools.

In the United States, students take many tests each year. Teachers use tests to see how well pupils are learning at school. If students pass these tests, they go on to the next grade where the work is harder. In this way, it is the students who are tested.

But these tests also show if teachers are doing their job. They have to give their pupils a lot of information in each grade. If they don't, their students may not learn enough. So the tests are also for teachers.

There is another special test that pupils take each year in all the schools across the country. It is a different test for each grade, but the same for all students in the same grade. It shows what they have learned that year. It shows which schools are teaching well. So tests are also for testing schools.

Most American schools give the following marks: A = 91–100 percent, B = 81–90 percent, C = 71–80 percent, D = 65–70 percent, E = 50–64 percent, and F = below 50 percent. In high school it is

possible to take some classes without marks. Then the student gets a "P" for "pass" and an "F" for "fail."

Teachers keep lists of students' test and homework marks. They give students marks for how well they work. Then they list the students' marks on their report card. Students get report cards four times a year. One copy is sent to the parents and the school keeps a copy.

Seventy-one percent of American students graduate from high school. A few graduate at the top of their class, as Jodie did when she graduated last year. She won a prize for her excellent high school work. The prize was money for college. She was among the 40 percent of high school students who go on to college.

Left: Taking a test.

Above: A student receives a prize at his graduation ceremony.

CHOOSING A COLLEGE

If you meet a group of twelfth grade students they are all talking about one thing: what are they going to do next year? Some students don't want to go on with their education. When they leave school they will look for a job. Other students are thinking about colleges. They are each writing letters to three or four different colleges, and sending in forms.

Colleges accept only those students who have done well in high school. They want to meet these students before they decide to accept them. Colleges want to know why students have chosen them, and how they will pay for their college education.

Students choose from about 2000 colleges in the U.S. Every school has its own special flavor. Top students may choose famous "Ivy League" schools like Princeton, Harvard, or Yale. They are the oldest colleges in the country—excellent, but very expensive. Other students choose large universities because they teach lots of different subjects. Some choose small religious colleges.

There are differences between colleges and the type of study programs they have. For example, many four-year "Liberal Arts" colleges are small and teach only the most important subjects for a general education. State universities are large. They teach many subjects and have some programs that last longer than four years. State universities are paid for by money from the state. Students from that state pay less to study there. Colleges are paid for privately, so students usually pay more to go there.

Whether a student chooses a small college or a large university, the cost of higher education in the United States is rising every year. Many parents find it too expensive.

Colleges and universities often have money for students who cannot pay, but it is not enough for everyone. Some have part-time jobs while they are at college. Studying and working at the same time can be very hard. But these students think it's worth all the hard work to get the college education they want.

Left: Yale, one of the "Ivy League" schools.

Above: The University of Wisconsin, a large state university.

GOING TO COLLEGE

Going to college usually means leaving home for the first time. Most college students live on campus, which is the place where all the college buildings are. Some have rooms in buildings called dormitories. Others may live in "fraternity" or "sorority" houses. These are clubs of men or women students. They choose their members carefully. Some students prefer to live off campus. They try to find rooms or apartments near the campus.

A college diploma is called a degree. There are three degrees that students can earn. The first four years of college gives an undergraduate degree. Students in undergraduate school study lots of subjects. They do not choose their most important subject until the end of undergraduate school. They earn credits for the classes they complete. They must have a certain number of

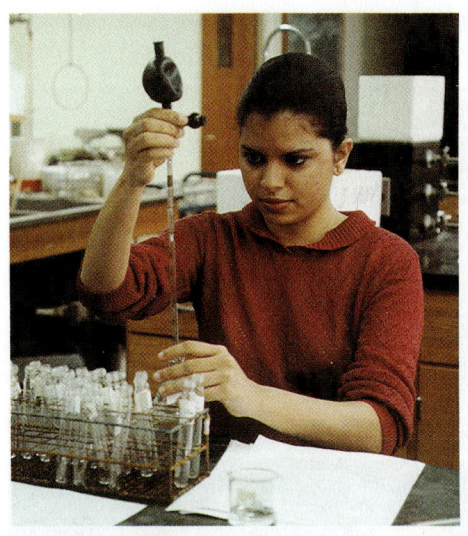

credits in their most important subject and some credits in other subjects, too. Then they get a Bachelor of Arts (BA) degree.

With a BA degree, college students can go on to graduate school. After two or three years, they can get a Master of Arts (MA) degree. They take only subjects that lead to the MA. These are subjects that will be important for their later work. Graduate school can prepare students to become teachers or lawyers, for example. With a Master of Science degree (MSc), they can become scientists. They can prepare for work in business with a Master of Business Administration degree (MBA). Students can go on in graduate school to get a Doctor of Philosophy degree (PhD). That is the highest degree university students can get. Most university teachers must have a PhD.

In the U.S., many students stay on at college to get a master's degree, because a bachelor's degree is often not enough to get the job they want. It can take a long time, and a lot of money. It takes at least ten years to become a doctor, seven years to become a lawyer, and five or six years to become a teacher. Many students are in their mid or late twenties when they finally start work.

Far left: A fraternity house.

Left: A room in a dormitory at Syracuse University.

Above: A chemistry student at the University of Maryland.

EDUCATION FOR LIFE

There are people in the U.S. who go to school their whole lives. In fact, more than half the American people go to school. Of course, children must go to school. But adults go, too. Some take classes after work. Others go back to school after they have raised a family. Some change jobs late in life. This is happening more and more every year. These adults go to college classes with the younger students and earn degrees there.

Joyce Connolly is older than most. She's fifty-five. She graduated last year from a small Liberal Arts college in Massachusetts. Why did she go to college? "I guess it's something I always wanted to do. I left school when I was fourteen. My parents didn't have much money, and I went to work in a factory near Boston. Then I got married, and with five kids to raise there wasn't much time. But I always liked books, and I wanted to study literature. I loved my studies, and I loved being with all those young people."

Certain colleges have night classes for adults who want to learn something new. A bus driver may take classes in photography. An engineer may want to learn to play the guitar. Adults often take night classes to learn useful things. These add to the quality of their lives.

Some people would like to study, but they have young children and they have to stay at home. They can take "correspondence" classes. The college sends them homework and tests through the mail. They can do the homework and take the tests at home. Then they send these papers back to the college. They can earn credits, complete classes, and get a degree by mail.

In the United States, about two

million adults are taking some sort of classes. There are many different kinds of study programs for all of them. Going to school is really a way of life for Americans.

Far left: Joyce Connolly and a classmate at their graduation ceremony.
Left: Computer classes at night school.
Above: New Americans learning English.

Addison Wesley Longman Limited,
Edinburgh Gate, Harlow,
Essex CM20 2JE, England
and Associated Companies throughout the world.

© Longman Group UK Limited 1990
All rights reserved; no part of this publication
may be reproduced, stored in a retrieval system,
or transmitted in any form or by any means, electronic,
mechanical, photocopying, recording or otherwise,
without the prior written permission of the Publishers.

First published 1989
Sixth impression 1997

Set in Linotron 202 Times Roman 11/13pt

Produced by Longman Asia Limited, Hong Kong.
GCC/06

ISBN 0 582 01714 9

Acknowledgements

We are grateful to the following for permission to reproduce copyright photographs in this title:

Ace Photo Agency/Gabe Palmer for page 22 (top),/Third Coast Stock for pages 12 (left), 13, 19 and 27. UPI/Bettman Newsphotos for pages 20 and 21. Colorific/© Jim Howard for page 29,/© Jim Pickerell for page 31 (left),/Picture Group © Michael Greenlar for page 28 (left),/Picture Group © Bob Mahoney for page 28 (right) and/Picture Group © Michael Grecco for page 31 (right). Glendale High School, Los Angeles, California for page 8. Sally and Richard Greenhill for pages 15 and 25. Longman Photographic Unit for page 2 (top). Photo Researchers, Inc/© Ursula Markus for page 17. Picturepoint Ltd for page 26. Tony Stone Worldwide for pages 14 and 22 (bottom), / Click-Chicago Ltd © John Lawlor for page 9 and /Click-Chicago Ltd © Michael Mauney for page 18. Zefa Picture Library for pages 5 and 30.

Additional photography by David L. Sanford.
Cover photograph by Images Colour Library Ltd.

We would also like to thank the following for their help in the production of this title:

Brighton High School, The Hartley School, National Bus Company; with special thanks to Brad Jacobs, Bob Joslyn and Emily Whitbeck.